AF615441

GIG AT THE AMTRAK

Joe Manning

First Edition

Flatiron Press, Florence, Massachusetts

GIG AT THE AMTRAK

Published by  Flatiron Press
575 Bridge Road, Unit 9-1
Florence, MA 01062

Printed in the United States of America

All rights reserved. No part of this book may be reproduced or transmitted in any form or by any means, electronic or mechanical, including photocopying, recording, or by any information storage and retrieval system, without written permission from the author, or his rightful heirs, except for the inclusion of brief quotations in a review.

Copyright © 2005
by Joe Manning
First Printing 2005

Library of Congress Control Number: 2004094377
Manning, Joe
Gig At The Amtrak / by Joe Manning.-1st ed

ISBN 0-9658684-1-9 (pbk.)

Cover design by Keith Bona.
Photographs by Joe Manning.
Front cover photograph: North Canaan, Connecticut.
Back cover photograph: North Adams, Massachusetts.
All newspaper articles are in the public domain, except where permission to use has been granted. The quotes from Letty Cottin Pogrebin and Elie Wiesel are reprinted with permission of the authors.

Printed by Proforma Universal Marketing Products, North Adams, Massachusetts.

About The Author

Joe Manning is a writer, freelance journalist, photographer, composer, lyricist, poet and artist. His book, *Steeples: Sketches of North Adams* (Flatiron Press 1997), is in its third printing. It has been required reading for several courses at Williams College and Massachusetts College of Liberal Arts. His most recent book is *Disappearing Into North Adams* (Flatiron Press 2001). In 2002, Manning contributed a lengthy essay about the social history of the River Street neighborhood in North Adams for *Porches: Art and Renewal on River Street*, a book edited by the Massachusetts Museum of Contemporary Art. His poems have appeared frequently in *The Berkshire Review*.

With collaborator Steve Vozzolo, he wrote and produced *I Love Baseball*, an album of new songs about the game. It is included in the collection of baseball music at the National Baseball Hall of Fame in Cooperstown, New York, and has been featured on ESPN. Their song about painter Norman Rockwell, "Norman Always Knew," was recorded by Arlo Guthrie and performed by Mr. Guthrie at Tanglewood in Lenox, Massachusetts.

Mr. Manning can be contacted at: Flatiron Press, 575 Bridge Road, Unit 9-1, Florence, MA 01062

E-mail: joe@sevensteeples.com
Website: www.sevensteeples.com

Acknowledgments

A very special thanks to:

Carole Manning, my wonderful wife of thirty-five years; and Sarah Manning and Ellen Manning, my talented daughters, for their love and support.

Keith Bona for designing this book and for his valuable advice.

June King, my English teacher at Calvert County High School, Prince Frederick, Maryland, for bestowing upon me a love for the language.

Carl Robare, my companion at The Bean, for his wisdom.

Lukas Previn (the composer), and Andre Previn (the performer), for the tune "Bye Bye Sky," which inspired my poem with the same title.

Gillian Welch and David Rawlings for guiding me through the Hilltowns with their songs.

Elizabeth Winthrop, brilliant writer and kindred spirit, for those long lunches at Brewhaha.

This book is dedicated to my ancestors: the Manning family, the Butcher family, the Chaney family, and the McLaughlin family.

Table of Contents

Toll Taker 47 1

Introduction: Discoveries 3
North Adams, Massachusetts 5

Seven Steeples 7
Steep Roads 8
Southview 9

Emigrants 10
Letter From An Old Settler 11
1842 Auction Sale 12

Things That Aren't There 13
High Rise 14
Elderly Housing 15

Mishicott 16
Fruits In Kanzas 17
To Our Friends 18

Empty House 19
The Mohawk 20
Old-Timers 21

Miss Alma Carlson 22
Escaped Captive 23
Grasshoppers 24

Strange Comfort 25
Conversations 26
Listening 27

Hank Mobley, International Jazz Figure 29
Gig At The Amtrak 30

A Female Stranger 33
Voices Of The Night 34
Man Adjudged Insane 35

Two Flights Up 36
The Hunter 37
Marcus Goes To Funerals 38

Switchman Killed 39
Tornado Of 1860 40

Tenement 43
Virgin Mary 44

Lightning Kills A Lover 45
Narrow Escape 46
Mule Team Drowned 47

Bright Windows 48
Kitchen Helper 49
Storage Bin 50

Abandoned 51
Seventeen Brought To Dubuque 52
Little Immigrant's Sad Lot 53

The Creative Mind 55
Where I Left Me 56
Clairvoyant 57

Assault With A Mop 59
You Are Shown A Way Out 60
Long Distance 61

Eagle Street 62
Furnace Street 63
The Hills Have Their Way 64
Ride To The Doctor 65

Marriage Announcements 66
Judge Elliott 67
Fire In Holly Grove 68

Open Mic In Milltown 69
Drive-Thru 70
Blackinton 71
Blue House On Brooklyn Street 72

Dauphin School 73
Spring Street School 74
Snake Problem 75

River Street Inn Previewed 77
The Golden Cross 78

Sunday Morning With Dog 80
Cell Phone 81
Bye Bye Sky 82

The Sea Bird Disaster 83

Final Autumn 90
Snowcap 91
Familiar Things 92
Mornings At The Bean 93
Other People's Memories 94

Hannah Maria Partridge 95

Reunion 96
Grandfather 97

Spruce Hill Lunch: A Farewell 99

Toll Taker 47

The only thing between us and the Bay Bridge
was Toll Taker 47.
That's what it said on his badge.

He peered in the window and said,
"You've got a beautiful wife."
And she said, "I'm not his wife –
not yet anyway."
And 47 pointed at me and said,
"What are you waiting for?"
And I said, "My change,
so we can get across that bridge."

And 47 turned around
and pulled out a stack of bills and said,
"Here's 300 bucks,
go get her a ring,
compliments of the State of California."

And I said,
"I can't take that money."
And she said, "Oh yes, you can,"
and reached across my lap and grabbed the cash.

And we felt like Bonnie and Clyde
in an old black jalopy,
as we left Toll Taker 47 in a cloud of dust
and disappeared over the bay.

Introduction

"If the family were a building, it would be an old but solid structure that contains human history, and appeals to those who see the carved moldings under all the plaster, the wide plank floors under the linoleum, the possibilities." -Letty Cottin Pogrebin, from *Family Politics: Love and Power on an Intimate Frontier.*

Discoveries

Many of us experience the sensation of driving the same route to work every day, and when we reach our destination, we have no recollection of making the trip. We can't remember passing a single landmark.

Like that trip to work, the study of history tends to be more about destinations and less about the little things along the way. But it is the mundane details of life that fill most of our time on this planet, details our descendants will someday wish we had documented.

As a writer and photographer, I try to spend as much time as I can carefully observing and recording all the seemingly uneventful stops on my journey through life. Extensive research of my family history has made me wish my ancestors had done the same.

In my poems, I try to speak in the voices of the people I have met or overheard, or in my own voice as a participant observer. The old newspaper articles and family stories that are scattered among the poems are just a sample of the many I have encountered on various genealogical sites on the Internet. They are like the scraps of life that wait to be found in the attics of grandparents. Some make me cry, some make me laugh, others just make me wonder. Like my poems and photographs, they are unexpected discoveries.

North Adams, Massachusetts

Many of the poems are inspired by my journeys in North Adams, so it helps to know a few things. This small city in the Berkshires is surrounded by hills that are dotted with rows of large tenements and Victorian houses, and the steep roads that wind up to them. And its incredible skyline of church steeples symbolizes the indomitable spirit of its residents. It is an unforgettable place, haunting and strangely beautiful.

North Adams had a thriving manufacturing economy until the 1960s, and finally lost 4,000 jobs and its largest employer, Sprague Electric Company, in 1986. The factory's twenty-six buildings are now the home of the Massachusetts Museum of Contemporary Art (Mass MoCA), one of the largest in the world. It opened in 1999, and is on target to attract over 850,000 visitors by the end of 2004.

In the 1960s and 1970s, an ambitious and unsuccessful urban renewal experiment was responsible for the demolition of more than half of the city's downtown retail and residential properties, and the forced relocation of thousands of persons. Most natives over 50 years of age are still haunted by the memory of the things that aren't there anymore.

My visits to North Adams always lead me to the warm comfort of the Appalachian Bean Café, a welcoming restaurant and coffee shop started in 1996 by Audrey Witter, a young social worker. Her first child, Hannah, was born two years later, and spent much of her first five years playing in the café and socializing with the old-timers in the morning. Often on Fridays and Saturdays, a local bluegrass group rehearses at a table by the window. The Bean, as locals call it, is a folksy cultural institution, where life in this quiet and gracious little city is played out for writers and incurable romantics.

Seven Steeples

I stood on the railroad tracks,
   stared south at the gray mountains,
And started walking,
   carefully avoiding the broken bottles
   and tangled weeds.

I picked up a rhythm when I figured out that
   one long stride equals two railroad ties.

After a while, I grew tired,
   so I turned around
   and started walking back.
I counted seven steeples.

Parts of red brick factories peeked over row houses,
   and around the corners of buildings,
   and down from wooded hills,
   and from across the river.
Big houses were stacked on cliffs,
   and it seemed a miracle
   that they hadn't tumbled end over end
   into a pile of lifeless sticks.

Now I know how it looked a half century ago
   to all the young men
   who disappeared into the valley
   on their way to war.

Steep Roads

Life is all struggle and triumph,
triumph and struggle.
That is why I love to walk
the steep roads of North Adams:
Prospect up to Franklin,
Meadow up to East Quincy,
East Quincy up to Kemp,
Hathaway up to North,
Cliff up to Charlene.

When I walk up these streets,
pumping my arms,
stopping for a breath,
exhilarated at reaching the summit,
turning around to the wonder below,
I walk with the thousands
who have walked before me.

With each step
I feel their struggles;
With each final ascent
I feel their triumphs.

Southview

I walked through the cemetery today.

It sits quietly in the valley;
the narrow road winds around endlessly
and down to the railroad tracks.
I wanted to see a train go by,
but they don't pass through here anymore.

I studied the monuments,
reading the names out loud,
musical, lyrical names:
McSheen, Dineen,
Larabee, Lamoureux,
Skovera, Luczynski,
Siciliano, Pettibone, Partenope;
People who came here on the trains
or in crowded boats
to work the mills and build their churches.

I drove back into town
and stared up at the steeples.

Emigrants

The names of emigrants who left Schuyler county in 1849 for California, as furnished by Jonathan D. Manlove, Esq., leader of the company. The company left Rushville on the first of April and reached Feather River on the 22nd of October:

John Blackford, Samuel Boring, Jacob Brickman, John Brickman, William Brickman, Stoel Cady, Barton Carrick, Dr. Clarkson, Samuel Clarkson, William Clarkson, Francis Dickson, James Doyle, Simon Doyle, Isaac Fisher, John Gapen, George Garrett, David Hindman, Samuel Hindman, Joseph Hurley, Isaac Lane, John Lambert, William Loudon, William Lusk, Jonathan D. Manlove, Marion Manlove, Thomas McCowan, John G. McHatton, John McNeilly, Elisha Moore, L. F. Moran, Augustus Peters, Marcellus Price, Jackson Reno, Clay Rogers, Mr. Rook, Mrs. Rook, Abram Ryan, Thomas Silvers, Edward Stevenson, H. W. Taylor, M. J. Taylor, James Teel, Francis Thorton, Abram Tolle, James Tolle, John Tolle, Mr. Weaver, William Weden, Charles Wells, Newton Witt, Charles Wolf.

Of the above, Dr. Clarkson died on a steamer on his return home and was buried in the Pacific Ocean. Samuel Hindman, Jackson Reno, Mr. Rook, William Weden, Marion Manlove and Thomas McCowan died in California. Isaac Lane died on the trip out and was buried on Pitt River, about 400 miles this side of California. Thomas Silvers died at New Orleans on his return home. Marcellus Price died at Alton, having almost reached home.

Francis Dickson and Edward Stevenson were murdered while out on a prospecting tour in 1851, by the Indians in California. In addition to the above names, three brothers, sons of Myron Gaylord of Round Prairie, went out the same year. One of them died there, another was killed by a grizzly bear while on a hunting excursion, and the other returned home.

Also Lemuel Sparks and son, Samuel Fisher of Brooklyn, and probably others whose names we have not obtained went out in 1849. Mr. Sparks has since died. Fourteen of the above are now residents of the county, nineteen are still living in California, the remainder are either dead or are now scattered in different portions of the earth.

-*Schuyler Citizen* (Illinois), March 2, 1859

Letter From An Old Settler

I was born in Tinmouth, Vermont, on October 16th, 1827. At that time there was not a rod of railroad in the United States, the first being built in 1828. When I was five years of age, my parents moved to Wayne County, New York. On August 29, 1849, I was married to Elizabeth Playford, who died three years ago last September. In the year 1850 we settled on the farm near Packwaukee, where I still reside.

There was not a tree touched by an axe up to that time. When we came to this part of Wisconsin there were no shingles, and roofs were made of shocks. There were no horses, and money was a scarcity. In winter, when we went visiting our neighbors, I would pull my wife and child on a hand sled.

At the time of my arrival, there were no railroads in Wisconsin, the first being built ran from Milwaukee to Madison and the second from Milwaukee to Waupun. At present there are four generations living on my farm, myself, Charles my son, Harry my grandson, and great grandsons, Elroy, Roy and Howard. I lost my eyesight completely four years ago but still have a fair appetite. I will be 88 years of age next October and believe that I am the second oldest man in the county.

N. W. Allen

-*Oxford Times* (Wisconsin), July 22, 1915

1842 Auction Sale

Having sold my farm and am leaving for Oregon Territory by ox team, I will offer on March 1, 1842, all my personal property, to-wit:

All my ox teams except two teams, Buck and Ben and Tom and Jerry; two milk cows, gray mare and colt, one pair of oxen and yoke, one iron plow with wood mold board, 100 feet poplar weather boards, 1,500 10-ft. fence rails, one 60-gal. soap kettle, 85 sugar troughs made of white ash timber, 10 gallons maple syrup, two spinning wheels, 30 lbs. of mutton tallow, one large loom made by Jerry Wilson, 300 hoop poles, 100 splint hoops, hoe, 32-gal. barrel of Johnson whiskey, 7 years old; 100 empty barrels, 20 gallons of apple brandy, 40 gallons of corn brandy, oak tan leather, two handle hoops, three scythes, one dozen wood pitch forks, one-half interest in tanyard, one 32 caliber rifle bullet mold and powder horn, made by Ben Miller, 50 gallons of soft soap, hams and bacon and lard, 10 gallons of sorghum molasses, six head of fox hounds, all soft mouth except one.

At the same time will sell my six Negro slaves—two men 35 and 50 years old, two boys, mulatto, wenches 40 and 30 years old. Will sell all together to the same party as will not separate them.

Terms of sale: cash in hand or note to drawn 4 per cent interest with Bob McConnell as security.

My home is two miles south of Versailles, Kentucky on McCoon's Ferry Pike. Sale will begin at 8 a.m. Plenty of eats and drinks.

J. L. Moss

-*Flemingsburg Gazette* (Kentucky), 1842

Things That Aren't There

I grew up in the produce section at Big Y —
  that's where my house used to be.
My sister swears I slept
  right where they keep the cantaloupes.

They tore everything down
  and took it away.
My parents couldn't watch.

There was this man
  who wouldn't leave
  till they shut off the power.
I rode my bike into town
  and there was nothin' but piles of junk.

I remember goin' with my dad on Saturday
  to the barbershop.
I'd hang around outside,
  then we'd go have a mocha sundae.
My mom used to take me to that shoe store
  with the flamingos on the wallpaper.
They had these big pink shoes,
  and I tried them on once.
She told me to wait a while
  and my feet would grow into them.

Last week
  my friend drove down from Boston
  and we walked around town.
I showed her
  all the things that aren't there.

High Rise

When I was in the sixth grade at Mark Hopkins,
  I used to walk down to see Aunt Bernadette after school.
She lived over by the Transcript building.
  Her apartment always smelled like cinnamon and apples.

I'd grab her hand
  and we would go down
  and look through the big window
  and watch the newspapers roll off the presses.

Aunt Bernadette liked to talk about Quebec
  and how she was going back there someday.
Then my parents sent me off to boarding school in Connecticut
  and I didn't get to visit her as much.

I came home for spring break when I was in college,
  and I rushed over to see her when I got off the bus.
They were tearing down all the buildings on Main Street
  and there were cranes and lots of men with hard hats.
It was weird how Aunt Bernadette looked so old
  and how her apartment looked so small.

She told me the city was gonna make her move.
  They finally put her in the high rise.

I work for a newspaper in Texas now,
  and it's a long way from North Adams.
I flew in last week for the funeral.
  Aunt Bernadette never made it back to Quebec.

Elderly Housing

I had my chance...when I was nineteen.

Earl wanted to go to California
  when we got married,
  but I wasn't sure,
  so we didn't.
He wound up at Sprague's,
  but he died before he could retire.
And now I live in the school
  I used to walk to every morning.
They call it elderly housing.

My window looks west on Route 2,
  and when I stare at the New York mountains,
  I wonder what would've happened
  if I had listened to Earl.

And so we eat at the dining hall every day
  and talk about the grandchildren
  and that nice young priest at St. Francis.

Mishicott

In company of Mr. Fischbein, of the Badger State Manufacturing Co., we took a drive into the country last Wednesday, directing our first to the village of Mishicott, where he made a short stop, and then proceeded to the beautiful and fertile farming region which lies to the north and east of that busy little burg. The farms located along the road which we traveled are said to equal any in the county in point of soil; and the tidy appearance of the barns and farm houses which we passed certainly indicated thrift and prosperity on the part of the farmers. We saw several fields of winter wheat during one drive which looked exceedingly fine. Most of the spring wheat which was up also looked flourishing.

The village of Mishicott is a handsome little town, and deserves a more extended notice than we are able to give it at present; but we shall endeavor to do it justice at some future time. It has good water power, a flour mill, a blacksmith shop, two churches, and a fine large school house.

Hitching our horse at the hotel of which Mr. Damon is the popular landlord, we gave that gentleman a short call. Afterwards we called on Mr. Heyroth, who is doing a large mercantile business there; on Selk & Son, who have a large store and are doing a splendid business, and on Mr. John Terens, who also has a large store and deals in hardware.

We looked wistfully over the river where J. Linstedt's large brewery looms up, but were unable to visit the vaults as we would like to have done had we had time. Mr. Linstedt has the reputation of making excellent beer, and from the sample we got at A.C. Teren's we should say that he deserves it. Mr. F. Zander owns a hotel in the village which is quite a popular resort, but for want of time we failed to give him a call, as was also the case with Mr. Braasch, who keeps a hotel and saloon on the southern outskirts of the village. We noticed several new buildings going up, which indicate that the village is neither dead nor sleeping, but full of life and activity.

-*Manitowoc County Chronicle* (Wisconsin), June 1, 1875

Fruits In Kanzas

When we turned our steps toward Kanzas, with a view of making it an abiding place, we hardly expected that during the season of fruits, melons, etc., we should find an abundance of such luxuries here. But in this section of Kanzas, at least, we can assure persons in the States, who are luxuriating upon the delicacies of the season, that our good people are scarcely less favored than they. For a fortnight past there has been an abundance of peaches; for a much longer time there has been a constant supply of watermelons and muskmelons, and those who enjoy good apples have not wished for them without an opportunity to gratify their desire.

The peaches here are the finest flavored it has ever been our good fortune to have tasted. They may not be so large and beautiful as the more highly cultivated kinds in the States, but they are large enough for all practical purposes, whilst their delicious flavor more than compensates for any deficiency in size, if from six to eight inches in circumference be considered rather diminutive. But the watermelons! – their size is only equaled by their richness. To find them weighing from thirty to fifty pounds is a matter of no very rare occurrence. The apples are not equal to those in the States, but we have not been advised of its being difficult to find plenty of persons who think them very good. And when persons get sated with these orchard and garden luxuries, they can go to the woods and provoke an appetite by wild plums, which are large, red and luscious, and wild grapes which hang in ponderous and purple bunches, tempting and beautiful.

To friends in the States, Kanzas seems a far-off and uncultivated land, but we can assure them that as regards these delicious bounties, this portion of the Territory is far from being beyond the pale of civilization. We regret that this condition is not more general. In a large proportion of Kanzas, the planting of orchards and tilling of gardens have remained for the white emigrant to perform, but here a dozen of more years ago the Wyandott Indians settled, and brought with them from the olden homes in Ohio, those tastes and habits there acquired, which now have for their results grain fields and orchards, gardens and homes. To these, the Indian pioneers, we are now indebted for many of the good things we enjoy. Our proximity to Missouri, also, enables us to draw upon her, so that our citizens may fare more sumptuously than they could have expected to when they started for Kanzas.

-John M. Walden, Editor, *Chindowan*, September 19, 1857
Source: Kansas Public Library, Kansas City

To Our Friends:

Customers, and people of Henderson and Adjoining Counties, Greetings:

The Nineteenth Century is rapidly drawing to a close, and the new one is rapidly approaching. This, the closing year of the century, has been one of unexampled prosperity. The earth has responded bountifully to the labors of the husbandman. Prices of all kinds of farm products have been and are now very remunerative. There is much to encourage everybody to begin the new century with hopeful hearts and bright prospects. None seeing the first year of it can hope to see the last one.

We might moralize and speculate ad infinitum, but that is not our purpose. We want to thank the people for the liberal patronage they have given us, and to remind them that we will still be at the same place with everything that is usually kept in a first class hardware store, as well as a stock of wagons, buggies, furniture, farming implements, cooking stoves, sewing machines, etc. We invite the continued patronage of the people, and will do all in our power to make it to their interest to trade with us the next year.

We wish you a merry Christmas and continued prosperity during the new year, the first of the Twentieth Century.

Respectfully,
Miller, Carroll & Spencer

-*Athens Weekly Review* (Texas), December 21, 1900

Empty House

Three stories high
  and six families short,
The empty house
  at the bottom of the street
  fades into its final century,
  while the big yellow machinery watches nearby.

For those who knew its dark walls,
  it is still a living house.

The sharp bang of radiators,
  the whistle of winter winds,
  the squeak of stairs under scruffy shoes,
  the sighs of a thousand long sad looks out the window;
They will not be carried away
  with splintered wood
  and crumbled stone.

For those who care,
  there is another house,
  up the street
  and around the corner,
  with plywood nailed across the windows and doors,
  as if blindfolded
  for the execution.

The Mohawk

I worked at the Mohawk Theater
  when I was in high school.
Mom always said I smelled like popcorn
  when I came home.
I saw *To Sir With Love* twenty-two times.

When I was a senior
  they tore down the block
  on the south side of Main Street.
I couldn't understand why my folks got so upset
  about a bunch of stupid old buildings.

When I got home from college,
  I landed a job teaching the seventh grade,
  and I'm still there.
They're trying to restore the Mohawk
  and fix up Main Street,
  so I took my class on a field trip downtown.
We walked up to the front doors of the theater
  and peeked in at the lobby,
  and I pointed out the old buildings
  that are still standing.
I could feel their blank stares.

Old-Timers

They're repaving Main Street today.

I round the turn from Eagle Street,
and as I walk past the Mohawk
I notice a bunch of old-timers,
each standing alone,
arms folded,
staring into the street,
oblivious to the noise
and the smell of tar.
They are lined up like parking meters.

I hurry down to The Bean
to get some coffee
and sit by the window.

I remember standing with my father
many years ago,
his hand on my shoulder,
as we watched the old buildings
across the street
disappear into dust.

Miss Alma Carlson

Miss Alma Carlson, the teacher near Colon, who was out in the blizzard for nine hours, is now recovering from the partial freezing of her feet and hands. She will lose the nails of her right hand and perhaps the ends of some of her fingers. Her right foot is still very sore, swollen and painful. After all, who has been braver than she?

She kept her little flock together in the school house until dark, and then started to her boarding place nearby for supper and a light. When she found herself nearly lost, a haystack was her only refuge.

She realized that to keep still was to freeze to death. So she commenced to pull down the hay and stamp it, and during those nearly nine hours she kept it up until those who passed afterwards said she pulled down nearly two thirds of the stack.

At one o'clock the gentleman at whose house she boards started out with a light to see if he could learn something about her and the children. For an hour he wandered about unable to find the school house. When he arrived there he found the children all right, but their teacher was missing.

This friendly light had, however, come to her rescue, for she saw it and stumbled along as best she could with her stiff feet, and as she fell into the door, said, "My hands and feet are frozen," and then fainted.

In spite of all this, Miss Carlson has continued her school every day. With a bandaged right arm and both feet in large "artics," she has gone on with her work to the present time. At 17 years of age, who can give a better record? When you count heroines, count Alma Carlson one.

-*Wahoo Newspaper* (Nebraska), February 10, 1888

Escaped Captive

Jane Proctor, who was captured by the Cheyenne Indians about twenty years ago, while on the road to California, is now stopping at the house of Norval Kelley, a few miles east of this place. She is twenty-four years old, being captured at the age of four. At the late fight between the Cheyennes and Kaws, near Fort Laramie, Jane made her escape, and came down to this region with the Kaws. Of course she has suffered a great deal, but was with the Indians so long that she became accustomed to their modes of living.

She has been sold often and has spent her time with various tribes, roaming over the country and leading a terrible life. Her brother, who was older, remains with the Indians, having married among them. Miss Proctor says there were always a number of captives with the Indians, and hence she has preserved a tolerable knowledge of the English language.

Miss Proctor thinks that some of her family lives in Southern Kansas, somewhere, and would like to have information concerning them. Her father's name is B. B. Proctor. Any information concerning him or any of the family will be thankfully received by her. We are indebted to W. T. Galliher, Esq., for the above particulars.

-*Emporia News* (Kansas), February 7, 1868

Grasshoppers

The grasshoppers are sitting on the stone walls earnestly watching the farmers sow buckwheat. When the crop is ready for harvest the grasshoppers will endeavor to save farmers the trouble of reaping the harvest. It is discouraging to see so many grasshoppers and hay, but half a crop. Farmers are reducing expenses of the farm as much as possible and trying to economize in anticipation of still harder times. Not much help is hired and wages are low. Many farmers are becoming silverites.

-*Stamford Mirror* (New York), June 30, 1896

Strange Comfort

There's a strange comfort
  in the gloom of this Saturday morning.
Staring down from the hills
  through a cold March drizzle,
  houses sleep behind dark windows.
The town is empty
  and I have it all to myself.
A bus pulls up;
  no one gets off,
  no one gets on.
Piles of gray snow
  lie in the middle of the street
  where flowers once brightened the late summer.
Suddenly,
  neon letters flash, "open,"
  and there is coffee waiting.

Conversations

Morning conversations in the café
  circle 'round the table,
  always coming back to
  dates on cornerstones,
  old photos in newspapers
  and the flood of '27.

Listening

Today is as gray
  as a cold cup of coffee.
The old guys fill up The Bean,
  but a little more slowly.

A train rumbles by in the distance.
  "Must be it's gonna rain,
  'cause I can hear the train."
No one even nods.

The coffee cups sit on the table,
  as still as the hands around them,
  and it starts to rain.

Audrey breezes in
  with wet hair.
"How you all doin'?"

No one says anything;
  this morning,
  everyone is listening.

Hank Mobley, International Jazz Figure

Hank Mobley, a jazz saxophonist of international stature who played with the leading musicians of the day and made his greatest impact as a member of the Miles Davis group in the 1960s, died Friday. He was 55 and had lived in Philadephia since 1972.

Born Henry Mobley in Eastman, Ga., he moved to the Newark-Elizabeth, N.J., area in childhood and studied music privately. Early in his career he played with the Paul Gayton orchestra and other regional bands.

As a tenor saxophonist, his most important associations in jazz were with the Horace Silver and Art Blakey groups in the 1950s and the Davis aggregation the following decade.

Later he was the co-leader of combos with Lee Morgan, Kenny Dorham and Cedar Walton. In 1967-68, he toured Europe, making appearances in London, Paris, Munich, Rome and other cities in Poland, Hungary and Yugoslavia.

Among the many musicians in his ken over the years were Dizzy Gillespie, Max Roach, Slide Hampton, Wilbur Ware and Philly Joe Jones. He played recently at the Angry Square on New York's 7th Avenue.

He was the composer of a number of jazz tunes, including "Breakthrough," "The Morning After," "A Caddy for Daddy," "The Dip" and "Straight Ahead."

Survivors include his father, Otis Rogers; his stepmother, Lillian O. Rogers; and two aunts, Jenethel Cooney and Rosa Boyer. Friends may call from 6 to 8 p.m. Friday at the Johnson Funeral Home, 46th Street and Woodland Avenue. Burial will be Saturday at Mount Lawn Cemetery, 84th Street and Hook Road, Sharon Hill, Delaware County.

-*Philadelphia Daily News*, June 4, 1986. Used by permission.

"I had a conversation with Hank Mobley before he died. Hank was a very prolific writer, but most of his songs were in different publishing companies, they're all over the place and he just didn't know how to get his money, even though he really needed it. At the end of his life, Hank was homeless; he was living in the Amtrak station in Philadelphia."

-saxophonist Gary Bartz, from the September 1995 edition of *Jazz Times*. Used by permission.

Gig At The Amtrak

I was rudely awakened by a man
   who set down his suitcase
   next to the bench I was sleeping on.
If it wasn't for all these travelers,
   I could get some rest.
I checked to see if my horn was there and
   found my left hand still squeezing
   the handle on the case.
I took out the horn and looked inside and
   there were still some notes left in it.
Some college kid with a guitar sat down and
   asked me if I played and
   I said, "A little bit I guess."

I saw two men come in carrying briefcases and
   wearing gray suits and it got me to thinking
   that it's a long time since I've been in a bank.
So I put my horn back in the case and
   went down to the biggest bank I could find and
   they were playing some stupid arrangement of
   "Round Midnight" on the Musak and it made me mad
   so I got out my horn and blew a few licks and
   then they told me to leave;
   so I did.
I'm always leaving places.

I hadn't eaten yet,
   so I walked back home and
   a train pulled in just as I got there and
   a crowd of people poured in
   so I pulled out my horn and started playing and
   two women came over and put some change
   in my horn case and I stopped playing and
   bought a Danish and a cup of coffee.

One of the women came back and asked me to play
  something by the Duke so I played "Sophisticated Lady"
  which I thought was sort of funny and I think she caught it.
Then her husband came over and pretty soon there
  was a small crowd and I imagined I was playing again
  with Miles and Trane and then I heard the change dropping
  into my horn case and I remembered where I was.
Someone applauded and then everyone applauded and
  some guy walked up to me and
  said I sounded like Hank Mobley.

I counted my change and
  went down to Tony's for a cheesesteak.

A Female Stranger

It was as "a female stranger" that she arrived at the bustling little port of Alexandria, Va., that Indian summer day in 1816, and it was as "a female stranger" she died in old Gadsby's Tavern, on the corner of Cameron and Royal Streets opposite the public square, when the ravages of typhoid proved more than the physicians and nurses could combat.

An intriguing tale, this, and one that has defied solution for these hundred years and more. Who was the young woman so obviously of gentle birth who was carried from the English vessel by her solicitous husband? Why did he stand in the darkened chamber at Gadsby's Tavern and demand an oath of those attending her that they would not divulge anything that transpired in the room of pain?

The unusual inscription marks the pretentious tomb erected by the bereaved husband in old St. Paul's Cemetery:

To the memory of a Female Stranger
Whose mortal suffering terminated
on the 4th day of October, 1816.
This stone is erected by her discon-
solate husband in whose arms she
sighed out her latest breath, and who
under God did his utmost to soothe the
cold dull hour of death.
How loved, how honor'd once avails the not,
To whom related or by whom begot,
A heap of dust remains of thee
'Tis all thou art, and all the proud shall be.

-*Richmond Times Dispatch* (Virginia), date unknown

Voices Of The Night

The woman's wrists were both laid back and open, all the tendons, veins, and arteries severed. How the woman cut the second wrist after slashing the first is a mystery. The cut in the neck is a jab on the side and is not dangerous. At the hospital, the woman was on the operating table two and a half hours while Dr. Moser brought together each separate tendon, vein and artery in the two arms which had been severed. It was a long and tedious piece of surgical work. Today it appears that Miss Goehner will live, although she is not entirely out of danger. A fairly sharp butcher knife was used in the attempt.

"The voices told me to kill myself," she told the doctor when he arrived on the scene.

"What voices?"

"The voices of the night."

-*Bloomington Telephone* (Indiana), December 2, 1929

Man Adjudged Insane

Albert Petterson of Eureka was adjudged insane in probate court here yesterday. About six weeks ago Petterson opened up a carriage and repair shop in Eureka and shortly afterward his friends noticed his peculiar actions in connection with business affairs. Two weeks ago he went to Wichita and opened up a similar shop. He was arrested there last Friday and brought to Eureka Saturday on a charge of fraud in a business transaction. He seems entirely unconscious of having done any wrong and maintains that everything will be all right. Albert is a bright young man and his friends would be glad to learn of his speedy return to health. The jury before whom he was tried was composed of Dr. Dillon, T.G. Mallicoat, C.M. Cheany and Elwood Marshal. Nine witnesses were examined and all told of deals and talks with Patterson which would indicate that his mind is affected.

-*Eureka Herald* (Kansas), July 12, 1906

Two Flights Up

The old man lives two flights up
  from reality.
He walks his dog every morning at 7:30.

I know,
  because I get a poppy seed bagel and a coffee
  every day at The Bean.
I always sit on a stool by the front window
  and stare at the houses on the hill.

Today
  the street is emptier than usual.
It's the end of June
  and the school children are gone.

The old man is late,
  but he finally comes by,
  wearing a dirty undershirt
  and a hunter's cap.
He tugs impatiently at the leash
  and scolds the dog.
The dog appears to squint at the light,
  as if hung over.

I go outside
  and ask the old man to join me
  for a bagel.
He just stares at me.

The Hunter

I saw a picture of the dog
  staring out at me
  from inside the newspaper box.
He was sitting in a pickup truck,
  looking sad and weary
  as beagles always do.

They found the old man.
  Rascal led them to his master,
  who was lying in the woods
  six miles north of town.

In the obituary
  there was a picture of the old man
  wearing a shirt and tie,
  but no hunter's cap.
They gave his address as 21 Eagle Street.

Two weeks later
  I went to his apartment,
  two flights up the dimly lit stairs.
His name was still on the mailbox.

Marcus Goes To Funerals

Marcus cuts out the obituary notices every day
   and rides his bike to the wakes.

He will walk in wearing a blue helmet
   and tight shorts
   and view the body.

Marcus will talk to the grieving family and friends,
   but no one will recognize him.
Later he will go to the church, kneel and pray
   and mingle outside with the crowd.
"It was a beautiful service," he will say.

Marcus will follow the cars to the cemetery
   and bow his head during the ceremony.
Then he will join the family
   as they quietly share an informal lunch
   at a relative's home.
Someone will ask him who he is
   and he will mutter something about being an old friend.

Somebody will get suspicious
   and Marcus will disappear on his bike,
   a sandwich and a piece of fruit in the basket.

Switchman Killed

About 10:30 Wednesday night, L. R. Shannon, a switchman, was run over by two Illinois Central cars in the yards here and almost instantly killed. There were no eyewitnesses to the accident, but fellow switchman, C. S. Atwood, was on the two cars that passed over his companion. He felt the jar to the cars, and when he reached the injured man's side he was breathing his last. The body was horribly mutilated.

The inquest developed the fact that the crew was making a drop switch to place two cars on the house track at the freight depot. Five cars were being pulled by switch engine No. 115. The third car from the rear was a flat car, and Shannon was standing on this car to pull the pin and cut off the two remaining cars to drop in on the house track. The train was going toward the switch and Shannon was heard to halloo, "All right," signifying that he had drawn the pin.

The engine and three cars pulled away. It was then that switchman Atwood, who was riding the cars in the house track, felt the cars pass over some object, and called the remainder of the crew to investigate. They found him lying beside the track. After the cars were cut off and the flat car had passed the switch, it was noticed that Shannon's lantern was on the car.

-*Clinton Daily Public* (Illinois), 1899

Tornado of 1860

The storm struck Lee County at about the center of the west line of Harmon township. It passed directly through Harmon and Marion townships, almost in a straight easterly direction, and aside from little destruction of fencing, did nothing destructive in either town. It continued its easterly course into Amboy township, but almost immediately it veered to the northeast and, passing to the north of the city of Amboy, it did the first real damage when it reached the farm of Michael Morse on the northeast quarter of section 9 in Amboy township. Here the buildings were demolished. Mr. Morse was badly hurt and his wife, Trial, and their daughter, Emma, were killed.

Continuing northeasterly, it reached the farm of Isaac Gage. In passing it shook the Linn house in which Mrs. Shaw was sitting, like a cradle, and the vibrations of that awful evening come back to her in all their awful realism, whenever the day returns to her memory.

Every building on the Gage place on the northeast quarter of section 1 in Amboy township was destroyed, and Ethelbert, a young son, was killed. Another son was injured so badly that he died soon afterwards. Another son, Luke, also was injured so seriously that he was an invalid for many years. A daughter, Helen by name, also was disabled for a long time.

At the same instant almost, the wind struck a tenant house just across the road from the Gage place, on the premises of Judge Lorenzo Wood, lifted it from the ground and never again did anybody ever hear of that house. Not a single board or splinter of all the debris was ever found or recognized.

The homestead in which Judge Wood lived was wrecked a little but not much. The tenants in the tenant building were spilled out, but not injured to speak of. The ceiling above in the Wood house was pushed down and it pinned down Judge Wood, who was lying on the bed, so that he could scarcely move; yet he was not scratched. The Peter LaForge house was hit next. His kitchen was cut off neatly from the main part of the house, but the damage was very slight indeed.

The Horace Preston place was visited next. Mrs. Grose was a daughter of Mr. Preston, and she went through experiences in this storm which come to few people, and she earnestly prayed that it never would occur to any member of her family. Upstairs, Mr. Preston said to his wife, "Go down into the cellar." Mrs. Preston picked up the little three year old boy and started downstairs and Mr. Preston picked up the little eight year old daughter Ella (later Mrs. Grose), and the four year old daughter, one under each arm and started for the cellar; but before he had advanced six feet the roof went off and he and the children, still in his arms, were sent sailing over the top of trees, and he landed on his feet in the garden, about 350 feet away.

Mrs. Preston held on to the boy, Horace, Jr., and was killed in her arms. A splinter was sent into the side of Mrs. Preston, which troubled him fearfully and ultimately took him off in death. In the cellar of the Preston house there were eggs, pans of milk, and other articles, but not one single thing was disturbed by even so little as a hair's breadth. The clothes of the girls were torn in shreds.

While visiting Mrs. Grose on Nov. 21, 1913, she brought me the family Bible, which was sent over the field a great distance and later recovered. This book sustained scarcely any damage, but another smaller book entitled, "The School and the Schoolmaster," by Alonzo Potter, published by Harper & Bros. in 1844 was so covered with mud that its contents were nearly obliterated, and to this day the mud sticks just as closely as it did the hour it was recovered.

A church was blown five miles. In the Preston house stood a stove, its top was taken off as smoothly as though removed by a cold chisel and sent half a mile away. A crock too was sent along for company, and it was not cracked. An iron kettle that Mrs. Grose owned was thrown into the well and into it was hurled a flat iron, yet the kettle was not scratched.

Between the Preston house and barn stood a strawhog house. When the storm had passed it was discovered that not one straw seemed to have been disturbed. The cattle and horses were driven away, but the horses all returned and the cattle were found subsequently and brought back home.

One incredible incident occurred on the Preston place which has been vouched for by many who saw it. A corn stalk was driven clear through one of the boards of the wagon bed. Chickens were plucked of their feathers, and the next morning the poor things were running wildly about the place until relieved of their suffering by shooting.

At the Daniel Frost place, next in its path, little damage was done. At the Martin Wright place the tornado did some very freakish antics. Every bit of the house was demolished with the exception of one part of the wall. On a couch against the wall, Mrs. Wright, an invalid, had been lying. While her sister sustained fearful bruises, including a broken jaw, Mrs. Wright was not disturbed.

-*Dixon Evening Telegraph* (Illinois), 1948
Contributed by the IL Trails Lee County Web site, hosted by Christine Walters

Tenement

I live in the narrow end by the bridge.

My kitchen floor is so crooked
  that the refrigerator leans
  and all the bottles and jars slide to one end of the shelf.

When the train comes through,
  it sounds like it's under my pillow.
Once my bathroom was so cold,
  my towel was frozen stiff.

But when the man with the camera came around,
  all he wanted to do was take pictures;
  so I took him up to the top floor
  and showed him the view.

Virgin Mary

The house sits across the river
   from the factory building.
It cries out for
   prayers
   and paint.

Amid the circle of flowers
   on the lawn,
   the Virgin Mary stands guard.

As I pass the house this morning,
   I stop and sit unsteadily
   on the guard rail
   and watch the sun
   stare a hole through the fog.

I imagine a proud old woman in the house
   sitting at the kitchen table
   among her statues
   and her photographs,
   while a kettle of tomato sauce
   steams on the stove.

Soon the sun will reach
   the front window,
   and I wonder if the old woman will
   open the blinds.

Lightning Kills a Lover

Upper New York generally gets a share of it whenever a tornado starts from Jersey up to the Hudson Valley, and it got a-plenty on Sunday, June 21, with a scourging wind, violent lightning and sheets of rain. One freak of the lightning was to strike a pair of newly reconciled lovers as they were kissing each other in an orchard in Tibbett's Brook Lane, Kingsbridge. The man was instantly killed, and the woman stunned and paralyzed. The man was Charles Fennelly, a big strapping fellow of 33. He met Louisa Costello about eighteen months ago, and they immediately fell in love with each other. Louisa, who is a fine looking girl of 22, worked in the Owl cigar factory, in East Twenty-sixth street.

-*Stamford Mirror* (New York), June 30, 1896

Narrow Escape

The little son of Mr. and Mrs. J.C. King, residing at 826 L street, had a very narrow escape from being killed by electricity last evening. The child and a companion were playing about Ninth and L streets while an employee of the Capital Gas Company was preparing the lamp there for night use. He had lowered the lamp to within a few feet of the ground, and after supplying it with carbons, returned to the street corner where the hoisting rope was fastened.

When his back was turned the King child ran over toward the lamp. When the man looked about the little fellow was lying on his back in the mud. Just then Mrs. King came out to look for her child, and learning what had happened picked up the unconscious boy and ran screaming with him to Peters Drug Store at Ninth and K streets.

There it was ascertained that the little fellow was not dead, as many had supposed, and Mrs. King's fears were allayed when assured that he would recover. The boy recovered consciousness in a little while and was taken home.

There is now such a wilderness of light, power, telegraph and telephone wires all over the city that parents should be careful to impress upon their children the danger of touching broken or hanging wires that may come within their reach, for electricity is a treacherous and a deadly thing to trifle with.

Nine-tenths of the adult population is also in need of instruction on the subject, for if a wire were to break and fall on one of the streets, the chances are that most men would thoughtlessly walk up and take hold of it, ignorant of the risk they would run of receiving a fatal shock.

Some of the poles are now carrying an enormous weight of wires, and some day the wooden brackets, or arms, are liable to give way, with terrible results. The only safe thing to do is for everyone to refrain from touching broken wires, for only trained electricians or linemen can tell whether or not they may be in contact above with wires carrying a heavy voltage of electricity.

-*Sacramento Daily Record-Union* (California), November 30, 1895

Mule Team Drowned

Frank Lorry's mule team was drowned in the Walnut at Harmon's ford last Saturday. Ed Keho was driving and barely escaped with his life. He did not know the river was up and drove in with the mules checked and straight across the river. After floundering some time both animals were drowned, but not until they had drifted almost to Speer's mill. The wagon and mules were drawn out and the harness saved.

The law provides that a gauge shall be placed at every ford, indicating the depth of the water, but we never have had one at any of the fords in this township. Soon after the mules were drowned, a wagon with men, women, and children was about to attempt a crossing and were only saved by the warning of John Harmon, who told them of the danger.

-*Winfield Courier* (Kansas), January 30, 1874

Bright Windows

The moon is full,
   and I am eager for this winter night.
I leave the river behind
   and walk on the hilly back street
   way above the city.

And then I notice this old Victorian house
   sitting warmly behind a snowy yard,
   glowing like a dying fire.
I stop and stare at it
   like a child.

I do not hear the woman screaming,
   or the man pouring his drunkenness on her,
   or the child sobbing under the covers.
The dry crackle of the cold air
   freezes me in the wonder of the moment,
   and I forget the darkness
   behind bright windows.

Kitchen Helper

I work at a restaurant over in Williamstown.
  I stuff the freakin' lobsters —
  five-fifty an hour.
Nadine waits on tables,
  takes home seventy-five bucks a night
  with tips and all.

I live on Eagle Street
  above the barbershop.
Sometimes my boyfriend sleeps over
  when he's not workin' nights at the factory.
He says he's gettin' laid off soon.

Someday I'm gonna get my GED,
  and then I'm outta here.

Storage Bin

My whole life is in a storage bin.

My lease ran out,
   and the landlord don't want me,
   'cause my baby's too noisy,
   so my baby's with my mom.

But I can't live with her,
   'cause she don't like my boyfriend,
   so I'm livin' with my boyfriend's sister,
   and my social worker says she can come up with the
   security and everything
   if I find a place.

So me and my boyfriend are lookin',
   and we hear there's this place over by Canal Street
   'cross from the gas station,
   so we're gonna go over there tonight
   and check it out.

Abandoned

A little girl seven years of age was found in the street at Buffalo the other night, having been deliberately abandoned by her father, who told her she must go away from home and earn her own living, as he could no longer support her.

-*Montello Express* (Wisconsin), September 7, 1867
Contributed by Joan Benner, Wisconsin Rapids, Wisconsin

Seventeen Brought To Dubuque

Mr. Robert Curran, accompanied by Mrs. E. Higgins, the matron in charge, arrived over the Milwaukee at 8:06 yesterday morning with a flock of orphans from the Catholic foundling asylum in New York. There were seventeen of them who alighted from one of the coaches and marched in twos to the Page house. They were taken into the dining room and seated at two tables. There were nine girls and eight boys in the lot. When they left New York Tuesday evening at 6 o'clock on a special car, there were 40 of them. Some were left between Chicago and Dubuque, 10 at Bellevue and various other small towns. They were neatly dressed, the girls in white hoods and neat, well made dresses, the boys in kilt suits and sailor hats, and all of them appeared well fed and in good health. Their deportment showed they had been well taught. Three and one-half years is the average of their ages.

These children came from an orphan asylum in New York City, founded by sister Irene, twenty-two years ago, and which has, up to the present time, found homes for 23,000 children and has made provisions for 8,000 mothers. There are at present 1,800 children at the home. Mrs. E. Higgins, the matron, who accompanied the children on the train, has taken over 6,000 children to the west. Mr. Curran goes from here through Wisconsin to find homes for another lot of fifty.

One little fellow, aged about four years, was given to his new foster parent, a lady from Apple River, Ill., who was in waiting for him. The scene that followed was touching. The lady hugged and kissed the little lad, and with tears in her eyes assured him that he now had a mother – a mother in every sense of the word she will surely make him. A middle age couple from Centralia took away twins, a boy and a girl, both beautiful children, and they would not part with them now for anything.

The agent says that this being a choice part of the country, orders are generally filled to meet the request of those who adopt these little ones. Of those here now, three go to Dyersville, six to Farley, two to Key West, one to St. Catherines, and the others to various other places.

-*Daily Times* (Iowa), June 9, 1893

Little Immigrant's Sad Lot

Little Alice Knearsey's story is a sad one. She is only 6 years old, and when she left her native land, Ireland, two weeks ago, her father, John, a stalwart young Irishman, seemed in the best of health. He had been on the police force in Dublin and had risen to be a sergeant. Then he lost his position, and with Margaret, his wife, and his little Alice, he decided to come to this country. Two other children were left with their grandparents.

The first night at sea a shriek went through the steerage of the Aurania. Ship's officers, crew and the passengers found Knearsey insane, standing over his wife threatening to kill her. Next morning the frightened child crept to the main deck and saw her maniac father struggling in a straitjacket. Mother and daughter passed a cheerless Christmas together. As the madman seemed better the next night, the straitjacket was partly removed. During the night the devoted wife crept from her bed to see her husband. The delirium returned to him in a flash and Knearsey attacked the woman. Three days later she again saw her husband, who was once more violently insane. The shock wrecked the woman's nerves and that night the ship's physician found her in convulsions. A few hours later she died.

Mrs. Knearsey was buried at sea, and little Alice, weeping and frightened, was taken to the cabin. A collection was taken up for the child and she will be sent back to Ireland.

-*Daily Iowa State Press*, February 10, 1899

The Creative Mind

The creative mind
  never lets you rest.
It goes on and on
  like an all-night diner,
Neon sign flashing
  Idea!...Idea!...Idea!

Where I Left Me

I went to California to find myself,
  but I wasn't there.

So I came home,
  and I was right where I left me.

Clairvoyant

Even as a child,
   somehow,
   I always knew that
   someday,
   I would be clairvoyant.

Assault With A Mop

Harriet Gully was summoned by Elizabeth Vowles for assaulting her on the 8th inst., at Wedmore. Elizabeth Vowles said they lived next door to each other. On the 2nd inst., she had her bucket under the shoot to catch rain, and the defendant came out and flung the water into the road. She told defendant not to touch it and if she did "she'd catch what for." Defendant dapped the dirty mop in her face, and knocked her across the shoulder. She did not touch defendant. Her daughter was in the doorway.

Robert Rogers said on the day in question he was in the lane opposite the house and he saw the defendant strike complainant twice with the mop and push it in her face. Complainant did not strike defendant.

Sarah Hooper said she was in the house with defendant. Complainant took three buckets of rainwater and defendant then put her bucket under. Complainant took it away and put her own there and dared defendant to touch it. Defendant was sprinkling the mop and complainant said if she sprinkled it again she would take it away. She did sprinkle it again, and complainant tried to take it from her. They had a tussle for the mop, but there were no blows struck.

Sentence was deferred.

Elizabeth Vowles was summoned by Harriet Gully for assaulting her on the 2nd inst., at Wedmore. Complainant said she went into the village after the row was over. When she went back, defendant's son came out of the public house with some drink and told his mother that she (complainant) was passing. Defendant came out and beat her about the head with a mop and after a time gave her daughter the mop and fell upon her.

Sarah Hooper said she saw complainant going back from the village, and defendant's son went into the house and told defendant that complainant was coming and she said "She'd go out and meet her with the mop." She did go and hit her several times, and then gave her daughter the mop, and tore complainant's clothes off her back.

Amelia Vowles, daughter of defendant, said her mother went out with the mop but did not touch complainant. She did not give her the mop. Complainant said she would go for the Sergeant and her mother said she would go with her, and complainant would not go. Defendant did tear complainant's bonnet a little.

The magistrates thought they had both assaulted each other, and fined them 2s. 6d. each and costs.

-*Wells Journal* (England), January 17, 1878

You Are Shown A Way Out

There can be no reason why any reader of this who suffers the tortures of an aching back, the annoyance of urinary disorders, the pains and dangers of kidney ills will fail to heed the word of a resident of this locality who has found relief. The following is convincing proof of merit.

J.B. Shuman, stationary fireman, Sodus St., Clyde, N.Y. says: "My kidneys acted irregularly and the kidney secretions were scalding in passage. I was lame and sore across my back and my skin was feverish. I had a dull ache in my back and mornings, especially, I felt lame. I used Doan's Kidney Pills and they gave me fine relief. They have also benefited me whenever I have had any signs of kidney trouble since."

-*Lyons Republican* (New York), September 28, 1917

Long Distance

The wonders of the long distance telephone are almost beyond belief. Recently the force in the Advertiser office, Montgomery, Ala., was enabled to hear some songs from Indianapolis, 700 miles distant, as plain as if in a hall.

-*Recorder* (Ohio), December 15, 1899

Eagle Street

I do not take lightly
  my walks on Eagle Street.
I treat them with reverence.

My eyes follow the curve of the Flatiron,
  the morning glowing
  on the dark green wood of a vacant storefront,
  the afternoon sun catching the top of the brick block.

On a rainy day
  the buildings huddle together
  like a family in an old black and white photo.

And the smells —
  bread baking at Molly's,
  hot dogs sizzling at Jack's,
  pizza on two corners.

At busy hours
  people rush by
  on their way to anywhere else.
At quiet hours
  I hear the ghosts,
  forgotten and invisible,
  like Eagle Street.

Furnace Street

Up here,
  everything is down there,
  and I have been looking down there
  from up here
  for a long time.

The river, the train,
  the gliders, the balloons,
  the baseball games,
  the fire engine, the police car, the ambulance,
  the trucks on the overpass,
  the smoke and steam rising from the rooftops —
Sometimes I wonder
  if down there
  ever looks up here.

The Hills Have Their Way

The hills have their way.

The three-story house
  sits high off the river road.
In a tiny yard,
  a rusty swing hangs near a ledge.
Steps lead up from the road to a stone wall,
  then to another stone wall,
  then to another.
Behind the third wall,
  a long wooden staircase
  climbs up to another three-story house
  at the bottom of a cliff.
Each house has a fire escape on both sides.

Neighborhood kids perch on the walls
  like pigeons on a roof.
A boy juggles a basketball;
  three times,
  it bounces away,
  down the steps,
  and into the street.
Each time,
  the boy patiently retrieves the ball,
  walks back up the steps,
  and hops on the wall.
A girl shouts repeatedly
  to someone in a third floor window.
The kids chatter and dangle their feet.

Mostly
  they just stare at the river
  and watch the cars coming down the mountain road.

Ride To The Doctor

The old man drives slowly up the steep road
  and stops in front of the yellow house.
The passenger door opens
  and a woman with a cane
  carefully gets out.
She turns and motions to the man
  to stay in the car.
"I'm all right, I'm all right," she says,
  and closes the door.

She climbs the twelve steps up the hill
  to the front yard,
  stopping at each one
  before struggling up the next.
She crosses the yard
  and climbs four more steps
  up to the porch,
  finds her house key,
  and goes inside.

The man drives to the top of the street,
  turns around,
  passes the house,
  and waves to the woman,
  who stands at the front window.

He continues on,
  his foot riding the brake
  all the way down.
At the end of the street,
  he stops,
  turns right,
  and crawls down yet another steep road
  on his way back into town.

Marriage Announcements

11 May in Portage City, Mr. Samuel W. Stimpson to Miss Alvira Smith, all of this place. We wish Mr. & Mrs. S. any amount of unalloyed happiness and prosperity as they together journey down the steep and rugged path of life, and may the 'little responsibilities' flock around the hearthstone of the worthy young couple in such profusion as to render their stay on earth as perfectly serene as a midsummer morning.

8 June, in the town of Douglas, by Jotham Pile, esq., Mr. Stephen Miller of Montello, to Mrs. Abagail Smith, widow of S. F. Smith. May their gray hairs turn to silken locks, their old age into youth, and the honeymoon last a hundred years.

-*Montello Express* (Wisconsin), 1864
Contributed by Joan Benner, Wisconsin Rapids, Wisconsin

Judge Elliott

Judge Elliott was a large-brained, large-hearted, open handed man, generous and brave, a true friend, a formidable foe, who never sought or shunned a quarrel, the idol of the people of his adored and adoring mountains. He was too noble to be untruthful, too magnanimous to be deceitful and too brave to conceal what he ever thought or did. These traits gave him great leadership with the mountain people, rendered him always powerful before juries and invincible with the people. No man who has died in our day has left a warmer place in the hearts of his constituents.

In politics he was a Democrat of the Jeffersonian school of strict construction, adhering to the teachings of the great apostle of liberty in favor of an economical government, honestly administered by public servants chosen for their competence and faithfulness, to the end that the people, free from unnecessary restraints or burdens, might enjoy the fullest fruits of their industry, never forgetting that the best government is that which governs least. Whether as Legislator or Judge, he was absolutely incorruptible and eminently self-reliant.

A true patriot, he loved his country; a true man, he loved his countrymen. No man could be truer to his friends or more generous to his opponents; hence his friends were many, his enemies few, his admirers all knew him. Possessing remarkably quick perception of the abilities and motives of men, he was a ready and efficient Legislator, and with an intuitive sense of justice, guided by strong intellectual powers and perfect fairness, he was a just and impartial judge.

As Judge of the Court of Appeals, he was courteous and fair with his associate judges, dignified on the bench and considerate of the rights of counsel and litigants. His opinions, published in 12th, 13th, 14th Bush's reports, are compact, pointed and emphatic. His ideas clearly expressed leave no room for doubt as to their meaning, and through all a great regard for precedent is shaded and controlled by strong common sense and ever present love of justice."

-*Daily Sentinel-Democrat* (Kentucky), 1884

Fire In Holly Grove

Warren Briteman, on last Thursday night after midnight, hearing a noise out in the barn yard among his horses and mules, ran out as quickly as possible to see what was the trouble and found his barn and crib of 200 bushels of corn on fire. His mules and horses were almost suffocated from heat and smoke. Briteman is a well-to-do colored man owning good property in Holly Grove and is highly respected by all the white people. This burning is attributed to an incendiary. Briteman is a tenant on one of Capt. Tom Mull's farms, but this barn was built at his own expense.

-*Brinkley Argus* (Arkansas), February 9, 1906

Open Mic In Milltown

Main Street,
  Friday evening.

I count ninety-six windows
  in the tall gray building;
  all are dark
  except one which reflects the half moon.

Two boys in college windbreakers
  hang out by the clothing store.
Several people shiver
  outside the ATM.

Three cars are parked carelessly
  in front of the art café.

Inside,
  standing near the Picasso,
  the poet recites to the empty chairs.

Drive-Thru

Seems like every town's got a Golden Arches.

You see a lot of stuff
   when you work here.

Every fall,
   they drive around the hairpin
   and down from the mountain
   lookin' for a place to eat.
They never even get out of their cars.

They see us —
   drive in
   drive up
   drive thru
   drive out
   drive on.

Blackinton

Standing under the railroad trestle,
I stare at the patterns of light coming through.
After scrambling up to the tracks,
I follow them all the way
to the old mill.
A horn sounds in the distance
and I run to the crossing
as the light on the engine
gets closer and closer.
The freight cars come and go,
one by one,
past the factory
where they once stopped.

Later,
sitting in the sun
on the steps of the old church,
I watch the cars speed by
and wonder if anyone ever bothers to slow down
to look anymore.
Tonight,
in the graceful house next door,
I will sit with friends
and listen to Schubert,
accompanied by the mysterious rumble
of a late night train.

Blue House On Brooklyn Street

The steep road winds up from the river
  to the blue house on Brooklyn Street.
The stream pours down to the river,
  flowing under the driveway
  of the blue house on Brooklyn Street.
Cats sit on porch railings
  and dart out from under rusty cars
  near the blue house on Brooklyn Street.

I wonder —
  Where did they get the paint?
  Who picked out the color?
  Has it always been blue?

Dauphin School

Dear Editor:

Our teacher has appointed me to write the news item of the school and community to you this week. Our school has not been very full for more than a week owing to the bad weather and so much sickness. We have about forty pupils in regular attendance and sixty enrolled. Fifty-five is the most we have had in one day. Mr. Tinsley Williams who was so low with black jaundice at our last writing is reported much better. Mr. Pierce's little child is still very low. Mrs. Jim Williams is still in bed with catarrhal fever. Mr. Joe Chriswell is very low with rheumatism. Mr. Allen Carroll who has been so low with pneumonia is better. Mrs. Buckner's little child died yesterday morning and they are going to bury it here today. Mrs. Rome Haunsel is very low with pneumonia. Mr. Tom Ellis who has lately bought land and settled a new home in our neighborhood has gone back to Mississippi. I have not heard what his sudden idea was for leaving. Mr. Bob Tanner is right sick this week. Mrs. E. Schrader is having a new house built on her farm adjoining Mr. J. W. Peay. I am ten years old and I am in the fifth grade.

Mr. Editor, if you will mail a few sample copies of your paper to our teacher, we will give them out and perhaps get some new subscribers for you. With best wishes for the Review, I will close.

Fon Gentry

-*Athens Weekly Review* (Texas), Janaury 18, 1901

Spring Creek School

Our school is progressing. It will be out by the middle of June. Health is very good except a few cases of pneumonia. We are having some good weather now. The people have most of their land broke. Some are planting corn. Grass is coming and cattle will soon be where they can live. This is a stock and farming country. Wheat and oats are fine. The old settlers think this will be a good crop year on account of so much winter rains and snows. I would like to hear from some of the boys and girls from Cross Roads and Phillips Chapel communities. This has gotten to be the best paper ever published in Athens. Remember just one dollar a year. Every family should read it.

Jason Langford

-*Athens Weekly Review* (Texas), March 20, 1903

Snake Problem

Monday, a little before noon, Mrs. S. H. Malcom discovered a snake lying in the middle of the kitchen of her house on George street, between Second and Third. At sight of her the reptile glided behind the flour barrel. Mrs. Malcom gave the alarm, and Alderman Ryan, who lives near, came in and killed the reptile. It proved to be a striped moccasin about three feet long. How it came there is a mystery. Considering the number found on our streets lately, the Council should pass an ordinance prohibiting snakes from running at large.

-*Alton Democrat* (Illinois), September 10, 1880

River Street Inn Previewed

NORTH ADAMS – In a row of Victorian houses on River Street, a new standard of industrial comfort is coming to life.

Early in the past century, mill workers rested in these structures after the labor of their shifts. Providing temporary refuge from supervisors and machines, the housing buildings sheltered people from the demands of the industrial age. Located just blocks from downtown, however, the houses also placed them close to the conveniences of the area.

Now, in a time defined by electronic commerce and new economies, some people believe the old ways of industry may offer escape. As renovations to the houses near completion and a new identity descends on the neighborhood, the buildings again may host a balance of past and future.

At the Porches Inn, a colorful reincarnation of 19th century River Street, staff members hope these rethought buildings will provide a perfect blend of retro-style and contemporary pleasure. Scheduled to open July 1, the inn is part of a growing initiative to boost the reputation of North Adams as a Berkshire cultural destination.

As representatives from nearby businesses learned on construction tours yesterday, the inn consists of four color-coded main buildings that accommodate 50 rooms and suites. Conference rooms will be supplemented by meeting space in smaller structures on the site. One small building will serve as a recreation hall, equipped with showers and change rooms for the outdoor hot tub and heated pool. A garden path will meander from parking to back doors and up the wooded hillside.

True to its name, Porches resembles a community connected by paneled decks, where life revolves around open spaces. Guest rooms open onto interior walkways that end in iron-railed balconies, where an upward glance reveals skylight ceilings. Inside many rooms and suites, frosted windows allow light to pass between painted bedchambers and immaculate white washrooms.

For $150 to $430 per night, guests may be entitled to such amenities as Jacuzzi tubs, wall safes, DVD players, minibars, high-speed data connections, computer and cellular phone rentals, breakfast service and museum passes. Upholding the theme of the inn, room service will arrive in shiny metal lunchboxes.

-Excerpted from the *North Adams Transcript*, May 25, 2001. Used by permission.

The Golden Cross

Gramma used to tell me about the floods.

She said that when she saw the store
  floatin' down the river,
  it was time to get out.
So she moved to Rand Street,
  'cause it was way up on the hill.

My parents lived on Front Street
  when I was born,
  so I was walkin' over to Gramma's
  by the time I was five.

When the war came,
  Dad went away
  and Mom got a job at Sprague's.
So we moved to 231 River Street
  where Gramma used to live,
  and then she moved in with us.

When they put in the flood control, Gramma said,
  "There's not gonna be any excitement 'round here anymore,
  but I guess that's good."

We used to sit on the porch,
  and I was always lookin' at that golden cross
  on top of St. Francis
  that peeked over Sprague's.
I would stare at it,
  and count how many times the clock tower rang,
  and listen for the train.

My friend Bertie took me over last week
to the grand opening of the Porches Inn.
She said, "I walked by there on my way to work for thirty years,
so I just gotta see it."

We sat on the porch,
and I stared at the golden cross, and Bertie said,
"No matter what they do,
River Street is still River Street."

All I know is —
I can't believe that someone is paying 300 bucks
to sleep in my bedroom.

Sunday Morning With Dog

Dim sunshine paints over the
  gray storefronts on Main Street,
  barely a block long.
One can look north and see
  a handful of old people
  standing in the churchyard.

A small dog sleeps in front
  of the drugstore,
  a stack of newspapers with a rock on top
  his only companion.
A gust of wind blows a few leaves
  across the street,
  and they settle on the sidewalk
  next to the dog.
He opens his eyes,
  gets up,
  and lays down again.

A noisy pickup truck with no license plate
  bounces to a stop
  in front of the drugstore.
The dog gets up and wags its tail.

A burly man wearing a fishing cap
  gets out,
  goes over,
  picks up the rock,
  takes two newspapers,
  leaves some change,
  and replaces the rock.
Then he hops into his truck,
  turns it around carelessly,
  and drives off with the door half open.

The dog barks twice
  as the door slams in the distance.
He finds his spot again
  and goes back to sleep.

Cell Phone

"Media rate," I said,
 "and I need a book of stamps.
My wife likes the ones with the pretty flowers."

Jamie weighed the package
 and tossed it into the bin.

I heard the familiar ring of a cell phone,
 looked around,
 and there it was sitting on the counter
 where Dave works
 when he's not sorting mail.

"Oh, someone must have left it here," said Jamie.
 "They'll probably come back for it."

It kept ringing.
 Jamie stared at it,
 I stared at it,
 the lady behind me stared at it.
"Am I supposed to answer it?" Jamie asked.

I thought out loud,
 "Could be some guy who's pinned under his car.
 He's trying to reach his wife.
 Might be his last call."

"That's awful," said Jamie.
 "What if it is?"

Then it stopped ringing.
 I put the stamps in my pocket
 And headed to the bakery.

Bye Bye Sky

The fragile melody drops in
  like the sun burning a hole in a cloud.
And then it is gone,
  only to appear once again,
  luring me into the elegance
  of its soft, drip-drop notes,
  before slipping off
  into a shadowy corner of my memory.

I hear it once again now,
  as I sit in the glow of a fading sunset,
The camera returned to its case,
  the last purple cloud lost somewhere
  in the bye bye sky.

The Sea Bird Disaster

The past week has been a sad one for Manitowoc. A calamity, the recital of which could not be listened to without a thrill of horror, had it occurred in some distant part of the country, has been brought to our very doors. Other great disasters have occurred on Lake Michigan, involving even more serious loss of life, and Manitowoc has happily escaped. But when the waters closed over the wrecked and burned Sea Bird last Thursday, a score of hearthstones in our midst were made desolate, and gloom and depression settled upon our entire community.

The first dispatch, received here about 3 o'clock Thursday afternoon, announcing that the Sea Bird had burned off Waukegan early that morning, caused unspeakable anxiety and distress, for a large list of passengers, many of them the heads of families and among our best citizens, had embarked on the ill-fated steamer. Subsequent telegrams were vague and unsatisfactory, serving only to confirm that the Sea Bird had been burned, and probably many lives were lost, and at 6 o'clock the wire, from some cause, refused to work, and no more messages could be received or transmitted.

It would be hard, indeed, to describe the excitement and anxiety that prevailed. The mental anguish and torture of suspense suffered during that long night, by those who had near and dear ones on the burned steamer, no pen can describe. The telegraph office, and the sidewalk in front of it, were crowded until a late hour by an eager and excited, yet patient throng, who watched and waited for further tidings until it was evident that nothing more would be learned that night, when they turned away with heavy hearts.

During the night the wire was put in working order, and the first message that flashed over it on Friday morning brought confirmation of the worst fears of the most despondent. Of between seventy and eighty passengers and crew on board the doomed vessel, only two were saved. Only two, and neither of these were from Manitowoc. But there was still left the hope, realized, alas, in the few instances, that some might have left the boat at Milwaukee or Racine; and the intelligence received later in the day, that James H. Leonard had been so miraculously rescued near Evanston, revived the hope that others might yet be saved. As the days wore by and no tidings came, this last hope gave place to the conviction that all, save these three were lost.

JAMES A. HODGES, Clerk of the Sea Bird. Was born in Taunton, Mass., and was 40 years of age. He came to Wisconsin in 1849, and was employed as warehouse clerk by Messrs. Kellog and Strong, at Milwaukee, with whom he remained until the spring of 1857, when, in company with Mr. Peter Johnston, he came to Manitowoc, and the two, for the six years following, carried on a general receiving and forwarding business on the North Pier, under the well known firm name of Johnston & Hodges. In 1862, Mr. Hodges withdrew from the firm to join the army and enrolled himself as private in Company K, Twenty-first Regiment, of which he was soon made the First Sergeant. He served with his regiment at Perryville and in other actions, and at Stone River was captured by the enemy and confined in Libby Prison. Upon being released, his health was so much impaired that he was transferred to the Invalid Corps, and was selected by General Sweet, Commandant of Camp Douglas, as his Private Secretary, in which capacity he served until the expiration of his term of service. In July 1866, he was appointed Clerk of the new steamer Orion, and remained on her until the close of the season of 1867. This spring Mr. Goodrich transferred the Orion to the East Shore Route, and placed the Sea Bird on this. At the request of Mr. Hodges, who wished to be with his family, to whom he was much attached, as often as possible, Mr. Thombs, clerk of the Sea Bird, changed positions with him. Of unquestioned business capacity and experience, his place will be hard to fill by his employer. Genial and warm-hearted socially, and generous to a fault, no one could make his acquaintance without becoming his fast friend forever after. He was one of the very few men who have no enemies, and will be sincerely mourned by all who knew him. He leaves a wife and four children, the eldest 13 years of age, who reside in the Second Ward.

GEORGE W. EMERY. Was born in the State of Maine, and was 38 years of age. Mr. Emery came to Manitowoc in 1856, and engaged in the grocery and provision business, opening a store on Commercial Street, and subsequently on York Street. In 1862, attracted by the promising prospects of the Lake Superior region, he closed out his store here and went to Marquette, Mich., where he engaged in shipping livestock and did a general merchandising and regular forwarding business. His family remained here, however, and he made frequent visits to them, and had several times made large purchases of livestock in this county in the way of his business. He was on his way to Chicago to contract for the shipment of goods to Lake Superior when he met his fate. Mr. Emery was a shrewd, enterprising businessman, straightforward and honorable in all his dealings, a firm friend, and an indulgent husband and father. He leaves a wife and three children, who live in the Second Ward.

CAPT. N.T. NELSON. Was born in Norway, and was 43 years of age. By occupation he was a mariner, from his early youth. He came to Manitowoc about 18 years ago, and since that time has resided here with his family, following his occupation as a vessel captain. He was on his way to Chicago to purchase a tug for use in our harbor, if he could find one that suited his purposes. Captain Nelson was an upright, hardworking, public spirited man, who was universally esteemed, and whose death is a serious loss to our community. His liberality was only limited by his means, and no worth object of aid was ever turned away by him empty-handed. He leaves a wife and seven children, who live in the Second Ward.

CAPT. JOHN SORENSON. Was born in Norway, and was 40 years of age. Like Captain Nelson, he was an old salt-water sailor, and was also a first-class ship carpenter. He came to Manitowoc about 19 years ago, and since that time has usually sailed during the summer and worked at his trade in the winter time. He had just sold his interest in the schooner Walhalla, but there was some mistake in the papers, and it was for the purpose of having this rectified that he was on his way to Chicago. He was an honest, industrious man, a good neighbor and a good citizen, and his loss will be deeply felt. He leaves a wife and two children, who reside in the Fourth Ward.

JOSEPH D. DOUCETT. Was of Scotch descent, and aged about 37 years. He came to this county some ten or twelve years ago to follow his occupation, that of lumberman, but a wound received in the service incapacitated him for severe manual labor, and at the time of the disaster he was keeping a boarding house for the employees of Vilas & Co.'s woolen mill, four miles up the river. He was on his way to Chicago on business relating to an application he had made for a pension. In October 1861, he enlisted as a private in Co. E, Fourteenth Regiment, and was subsequently promoted to be a corporal, and detailed as one of the regimental color guard. At the battle of Corinth, in October 1862, while his regiment was being driven from its position by the overwhelming numbers of the enemy, Doucett, in endeavoring to save the colors from capture, was borne to the ground by a bayonet thrust, and left for dead on the field. He was taken and cared for by the enemy, and when he recovered and returned to his friends in the January following, was welcomed as one from the dead. Always prompt and faithful in the execution of his duty, brave even to rashness, and upright and honorable as a man, the army rolls do not contain the name of a better soldier than was Joe Doucett. May his memory be ever green. He leaves a wife and two children, who live near Vilas & Co.'s mill.

JAMES LEYKOM. Has lived in Manitowoc with his parents since his early boyhood, was a shoemaker by occupation, and had just completed his 21st year. He was on his way to Chicago to care for his brother, John R. Leykom, who has been ill for several weeks past, when, just on the threshold of manhood, he met his sad fate. He was a young man of correct principles and much promise, and was highly esteemed by all who knew him. His father's family reside in the Third Ward.

PATRICK C. DENAHAE. Was born in Ireland, and was 28 years of age. He came to America when but 11 or 12 years old, with his parents, who moved to this county a few years later. In 1862, he went to Chicago and engaged in business, where he had continued since, and prospered; and only last May the Pilot announced his marriage with a daughter of Mr. Michael Doolan, of this village. With every prospect of a long life of happiness before them, he has been suddenly deprived of existence and a shadow cast up her young life for all time. Mr. Denahae intended returning to Manitowoc to live, and brought with him from Chicago about $1200 to purchase a lot he had fixed upon near the corner of Buffalo and Ninth streets. The property was sold, however, before his arrival, and this money was on his person at the time of the disaster. He was a generous, warm-hearted young man, and his untimely death is lamented by a large circle of friends. His wife, and an infant child, but a few weeks old, are with her parents, in the Second Ward.

FRANZ KLIMMER. Was an old resident of Manitowoc, and aged about 50 years. About a year ago he sold his farm, just out of town on the Calumet road, and went to Chicago to go into business with a son-in-law. He came to Manitowoc for the balance of the money, due on his farm, which he got and left with his son-in-law here, Mr. Haegen, but had about $500 on his person when lost. He leaves a wife and two married daughters.

WENZEL HAVLICHEK. Lived in the town of Mishicott, was 26 years of age and a farmer by occupation. He leaves a wife and three children.

CASPAR LEGRO. Lived in the town of Mishicott, was 21 years of age, a farmer and a single man.

ALBERT MRWA. Lived in the town of Mishicott, was 25 years of age, a laborer and a single man.

HENRY PFEFFER. Was a young man, 21 or 22 years of age, and unmarried. He was the keeper of the tavern on the corner of Main and Marshall streets, nearly opposite the Catholic church. He had business in Milwaukee, but concluded to go on to Chicago, for company, with James Leykom, between whom and himself there existed a strong friendship. He leaves a widowed mother.

CHARLES RIECHEN. Was about 40 years of age, and had been a resident of Manitowoc for the past 12 years. He was the master carpenter in Goodrich's shipyard here, and was highly esteemed by those who knew him. He leaves a wife and one child, who live on the South side.

FRED HENNING. Was a single man about 20 years of age. He lived in the town of Newton.

R.H. HUNT. Had been in Manitowoc only about three weeks, and was on his way to his home in Leonidas, Mich. He was 32 years of age, and, we believe, leaves a family.

WILLIAM BARTER. Had made it his home here for a year past, was about 40 years of age, and a single man. He was a brother-in-law of Mr. Cox, of this village, and was on his way to Chicago to work at his trade, painting. During his stay here he made many friends who will regret his death.

AUGUST WILDE. Was 19 years of age, and a shoemaker by occupation, but shipped as a deck hand. His father and mother live near Klimmer's farm, on the Calumet road.

AMOS MYER. Was about 21 years of age, and has lived here 14 or 15 years. Was working as a deck hand on the steamer. His mother and stepfather live here.

FRED FLOSBACH. Was 18 years of age, has a mother and brothers and sisters living here. Was formerly employed in the Nord Westen office, and had shipped as a deck hand.

HENRY NIEMAN. Was about 20 years of age, and had shipped as a deck hand. His father died about four years since, and upon him has since devolved the support of his widowed mother and younger brothers and sisters, to whom his loss will be irreparable. Those acquainted with the family speak of him in terms of the highest praise. He was honest and industrious, a dutiful son and an affectionate brother.

JOHN FOUCKS. Was about 19 years of age and a deck hand. Has friends on the South side.

MISS TERENE OLESON. Was born in Norway, and was aged about 33 years. Had been employed in Mr. J.C. Johnson's tailoring establishment, and was on her way to Chicago to visit some friends. Miss Oleson came over from the old country only last year.

JOHN WALLA and his wife ROSALIE, with their four children, took passage on the steamer here, intending to go to Nebraska to buy a farm. They were Bohemians, only arrived from the old country last fall, and had been living during the winter in the town of Mishicott. At Milwaukee, Mr. Walla got off and went up into the city to see a sister who lives there and when he returned the boat was gone. His life was thus spared, but his wife and four children, the eldest a boy 16 years of age, were all lost.

The above, so far as we have been able to learn, includes all who embarked on the ill-fated steamer at this port who have not since been heard from. To the bereaved ones, whose firesides have been thus rudely desolated, will go out the earnest and heart-felt sympathies of all; but their grief is beyond the reach of human sympathy. Let us trust that He who tempereth the wind to the shorn lamb will, in His own good time, assuage their sorrow, and that they may, in time, even find a sweet though sad pleasure in recalling to memory the virtues of their loved ones, who are "not lost, but gone before."

-*Manitowoc Pilot* (Wisconsin), April 17, 1868

Final Autumn

The gold letters,
  faded as the fallen leaves of a Halloween oak,
And the red sign,
  darkly brilliant as a Columbus Day maple,
Are carefully removed
  from the weary façade of another time,
In this final autumn
  of the five and dime.

Snowcap

There's a change on the mountains this morning.

The trees are bare;
  on the hill
  I see houses
  that seem to have sprung up overnight.

The wind runs up River Street
  and the river runs with it;
  it runs cold.
I walk with my head down
  and my hands in my pockets.
When I cross the bridge,
  I don't even stop
  to look back at the city.

When I reach Main Street,
  the sun glows on the red brick
  and I spot the snowcap on Florida Mountain.
I feel a sudden rush,
  and I want to tell somebody,
  but there's no one around.

Familiar Things

The morning DJ is talking about an arctic air mass
as I drive down Main Street
and park in front of The Bean.
On the mountain
a few trees are already red and yellow.
The cold wind sweeps me inside,
and I take my seat by the window.

Boys in baggy pants
chew gum
and shout at the girls
on their way to school.
The old man goes by
wheeling his dog in a shopping cart.
A student driver
darts out of Holden Street
and nearly makes a left turn into traffic.
Audrey bounces in
from across the street
and greets her customers
with a smile as fresh as a hot bagel.

The sun breaks through the heavy sky,
and I am grateful
for familiar things.

Mornings At The Bean

Another glorious dawn
  follows me over the mountain,
  down to the valley,
  and into The Bean.

At Tony's table by the window,
  Eric and the gang
  play a sweet fiddle tune.
At another table,
  Ziggy and Ron and Tommy
  laugh and chatter and pick on Audrey.
She just smiles —
  she is always smiling.

Little Hannah smiles that same smile,
  as she circles 'round on her tricycle,
  then climbs up on the chair next to Carl.
Her world is full of old men
  who drink coffee.
Like her mother,
  she will grow up loving people and life
  in this quiet and gracious little city.

Other People's Memories

Wherever I walk in this city,
  I am followed by other people's memories,
  making me nostalgic
  for streets and buildings I never saw,
  friends I never knew,
  and the good old days I never lived through.

Hannah Maria Partridge

Hannah Maria Partridge was born January 2, 1804, in St. Martin, Birmingham, Warwick, England; and she died September 17, 1893, in Douds, Van Buren County, Iowa.

She married three times, to her first husband, John Nutt on July 5, 1830, in County of Warwick, England. He died about December 1842 in Van Buren County, Iowa. Their children were Jhon Fredrick, born 1831 in England; Thomas James, born 1833 in England; Owen, born 1834 in England; Alfred, born 1836 in England; Clarissia, born 1838 in England; Edmun William, born 1840 in England, and Edward Rueben, born 1843 in America.

Jhon Fredrick died before 1841 in England; Thomas James died in 1862 in the War of the Rebellion of 1861; Owen died in 1897 in Douds, Iowa; Alfred died between 1841 and 1850 in America; Clarissia died between 1860 and 1870 in America; Edmun William died before 1850 in America; and Edward Rueben died between 1850 and 1860 in America.

Hannah and her five children came to America, June 8, 1841, on the Ship Denmark, landing in New Orleans, Louisiana. She then traveled up the Mississippi by steamboat to join her husband, Mr. Nutt, at Keokuk, Iowa. John died a year later.

Hannah Maria next married John Digger Mansell on Oct 3, 1844. This marriage wasn't to last. He took her money, some of her property, and she was left to depend on neighbors to help her. She filed and received the first recorded divorce in the state of Iowa. Hannah divorced John Mansell on June 14, 1845, and the story goes that her friends and neighbors tied him to a raft and sent him down river.

She married her third husband, John Beale, on August 4, 1846, in Van Buren County, Iowa. Hannah and John had one child, John Walker Beale, born in 1847.

-Contributed by Bobbi Senior, from the line of John Walker Beale.

Reunion

It used to snow
when we were kids,
all day, waist deep, pure white.

It would start with a few flakes
here and there
and grow into a windy swirl.

When I saw you
for the first time in forty years,
I remembered the snow,
You waiting at the top of the hill,
my eyes fixed on yours
as I pulled the sled behind me.

Grandfather

My mother crumbled
  under the weight
  of his grumbling words,
But I remember
  sharing his silence
  when Mozart played.

Townsfolk were annoyed
  at his careless wanderings on private roads,
But I remember
  discovering new places
  on a Sunday drive.

I remember his violin,
  his musical hands,
  and dancing together to *Peter And The Wolf*
  in his enormous living room,
Hot chocolate on Saturday mornings
  at Woodburn's Restaurant,
  and riding around all day
  making up silly songs.

Children —
  when I lead you astray on country roads,
  Grandfather is to blame.
When I hide in my room with Beethoven,
  Grandfather is to blame.
When we dance together to *Peter And The Wolf*
  in the living room,
  Grandfather dances with us.

Spruce Hill Lunch: A Farewell

"The past is never dead. It's not even past."
-William Faulkner

I grew up in Dowell, Maryland, a town so small that you didn't need a phone very often, because everyone you knew (or needed to know) was within hollering distance. Dowell was just a few houses on one side of a wide creek, a combination post office/general store, and a tavern. We did all of our business in Solomons Island, a town of about 800 people just down the road on the Patuxent River.

Solomons is where my father worked as a marine biologist, where my mother worked as a librarian, and where my brother and I attended elementary school. It's also where we played Little League and Babe Ruth League baseball, where we went to the movies on weekends (one of the theaters was on a long pier), and where most of my playmates were a 15-minute bike ride away. It didn't occur to me at the time, but I guess it was not too far short of an idyllic place for a kid to live.

My maternal grandmother, Maggie Belle McLaughlin, also grew up in a rural environment, one she might have regarded nostalgically as equally idyllic. She was born 126 years ago in Spruce Hill, Pennsylvania, a tiny agricultural village in the Tuscarora Valley, about 35 miles northwest of Harrisburg. She lived in a large stone house that was apparently built around the time her father, John A. McLaughlin, was born (1834). Thirty years later, John fought in the Civil War as a member of the 101st Regiment of Pennsylvania volunteers. After the war, he married Hannah Jane Butler and spent the rest of his life working as a farmer.

Maggie McLaughlin attended Marshall Academy (now Marshall University) in Huntington, West Virginia. After living and working in Huntington for a few years, she met and married Maryland native and building contractor Conrad Marene Chaney, and they raised a family (including my mother Mary Elizabeth) in Washington, DC.

My mother loved to talk about her extended family visits to Spruce Hill when she was a little girl. Her Aunt Myrtle lived just across the road from the stone house, and there were several families nearby with kids to play with, a little general store in which to hang out and buy candy, and a church several miles away in a village called Academia. I visited once with my parents around 1950, when I was about nine years old, and all I can remember is that the house was big, and that Aunt Myrtle made ice cream in a bucket on the back porch.

In May 2003, my wife and I drove down from our home in Northampton, Massachusetts, to visit my mother in Maryland, and we took her up to Spruce Hill. She hadn't been there in more than 50 years. Having gone back to several of my family homes over the years, I expected the shock and disappointment that comes with discovering that progress and faded memories have rendered once-familiar things as practically unrecognizable.

Just north of Baltimore, we got off the beltway and headed northwest on a two-lane road that rolled through little valley hamlets, and then to Hanover, a factory town where they make Utz Potato Chips. After we reached Carlisle, a college town that reminded me of Northampton, we wound our way up and down several mountain passes before finally descending into Spruce Hill.

Right away, we found the stone house. It looked exactly like my mother had described it. And right across the street was Aunt Myrtle's house, though it seemed a lot more modest than I remembered. Along the same road, we passed by Store Lane, aptly named, because that's where the general store still stands. It was vacant. We even saw the one-room schoolhouse that Maggie Belle McLaughlin attended in the 1880s. It's now someone's home.

As we drove around, my mother kept coming up with new and tantalizing facts and stories I had never heard before. Seeing the green Tuscarora

Mountains to the east, and the valley dotted with farms and beautiful stone barns, we could ascertain pretty quickly that there would be no malls or highways to spoil the landscape or the memories. Almost nothing had changed in 50 years. In fact, except for the blacktop roads and telephone poles, the area probably looked much like it did 150 years ago.

Unable to locate the church and cemetery in Academia where my mother's grandparents are buried, we drove into Port Royal, which is two miles north of Spruce Hill, and asked for directions at the post office. After pointing us in the right direction, the clerk recommended that we stop the following morning at Spruce Hill Lunch, where the locals and old-timers hang out.

After a night at the Super 8 in Lewistown, we pulled up in the parking lot of Spruce Hill Lunch around mid-morning. About a mile north of my grandmother's stone house, the restaurant is located in a quaint building that looks a little like a train station. It was built in the 1940s, so it was new to my mother. She and my wife went in while I stayed outside and took a few pictures.

When I finally came through the door, my mother was sitting on a stool talking to a lady behind the counter. They were all smiles. At a table nearby, two couples looked on with amazement as they dug into a big breakfast. The lady was owner Carlen McClure, and she seemed to know something about nearly everyone my mother ever knew in Spruce Hill. Almost immediately, Mom was the center of attention, as others joined in the conversation, including whoever happened to walk in and wonder what was going on.

Carlen was, of course, a native, and she was excited to be able to compare notes with my mother about the people and the history of Spruce Hill. After a good 90 minutes of this, she extended an invitation for a return visit ("Come in the fall. It's beautiful then. I'll take you on a tour and cook you dinner.").

Spruce Hill Lunch was full of local color and good cheer. And it was decorated with historic photos and hundreds of curios like old soda bottles and cracker tins. The food was wonderful, especially the homemade pies. Then we headed for the cemetery. As we drove over to Academia, I thought to myself, "In another generation, will this country still have small towns and places like Spruce Hill Lunch where local folks will not only welcome visitors looking for their roots, but will also recognize and remember the family names?"

At the cemetery, we spotted my mother's family gravesite just a few steps up the hill from where we parked. There we were, my mother and I, standing next to the headstones of my great-grandparents. It seemed appropriate that clouds hung low on the mountains and a light drizzle filled the cool spring air. The McLaughlin family emigrated from Ireland in the 1700s, and there was an eerie Celtic spirit to that memorable day.

Mary Elizabeth Manning passed away on January 22, 2004, at the age of 85.

"The act of writing is for me often nothing more than the secret or concious desire to carve words on a tombstone: to the memory of a town forever vanished, to the memory of a childhood in exile, to the memory of all those I loved and who, before I could tell them I loved them, went away."
-Elie Wiesel, from *Legends of Our Time*

ALSO FROM THE AUTHOR

Steeples is a unique snapshot of North Adams as it begins the transition from a declining mill town to a center for contemporary art. Through a blend of oral histories, photographs, and poetry, the author portrays this quiet little city in the Berkshires, as its people remember the good old days and await the opening of the Massachusetts Museum of Contemporary Art (MASS MoCA) in 27 factory buildings left vacant in 1986 by the Sprague Electric Company. The story of the city and its immigrant people is told through the oral histories, which will remain a valuable document as memories fade with time. The photographs show the city as it was, as it is now, and as it may never be again. The poetry evokes the stillness and nostalgia of a quiet Main Street and the beauty of the geographical setting in the Berkshire Mountains.

Quotes From Reviews

"Joe Manning goes right to the heart and soul of a town. On the surface, ***Steeples*** *is a book about North Adams; but it is much more. It is a book that honors history, the people that live it, and the ways in which they are inextricably intertwined."*
-Elizabeth Winthrop, author of over fifty works of fiction for adults and children, including *Dog Show, Island Justice*, *The Castle in the Attic* and *Dumpy La Rue*

*"***Steeples*** is a splendid book. Wise, engaging, and informative, it provides a wonderful bridge between North Adams as it was and the place we see today. Manning has caught both the spirit and the richly complex character of its past better than anything that has ever been written about the subject."*
-Robert F. Dalzell, Ephraim Williams Professor of History at Williams College, and author of numerous books and articles on early American history

*"***Steeples*** is an evocation of something that has been lost in the heart of America. I find the interviews very moving. I am impressed with the photographs and the richness of the urbanism that they evoke."*
-James Howard Kunstler, author of *The Geography of Nowhere*

"Joe Manning uses interviews, his own poems, and photographs to tell the story of the city of North Adams and its struggle to maintain its history. The interviews tell a very personal story, one which Manning obviously has invested himself in. A very original historical work."
-Historical Journal of Massachusetts

***"Steeples** is a wonderful document, one students could use as a model to preserve (or simply perceive) some of the wonders of their own localities."*
-Eric Oatman, Editorial Director, *Weekly Reader*

"Every American town should be fortunate enough to have a chronicler as devoted and creative as Joe Manning. After reading the funny, tragic, and insightful interviews, you may feel that you know these people, almost as if they were your own neighbors."
-Roadside Magazine

How To Order *Steeples*

Cost: $22.95 (price includes shipping).
Make check payable to Joe Manning.
Send to:
Joe Manning, Flatiron Press
575 Bridge Rd, Unit 9-1
Florence, MA 01062.

All orders shipped Media Mail via US Postal Service.
For other shipping options, call or email the author.

Phone: 413-584-0679
Email: joe@sevensteeples.com
Website: www.sevensteeples.com

*Ten percent of the gross sales of this book is donated to the North Adams Public Library.

ALSO FROM THE AUTHOR

Disappearing Into North Adams takes readers on a journey from the destructive urban renewal program in downtown North Adams, Massachusetts, in the 1960s and 1970s, to the closing of the huge Sprague Electric factory in 1986, to the opening of the Massachusetts Museum of Contemporary Art (MASS MoCA) in the Sprague complex in 1999. Through the lively, heartwarming, and often funny interviews with residents, old and young; the nostalgic archival photographs; the author's insightful essays and poetry; and his own impressionistic snapshots, the sad but ultimately uplifting story of the rebirth of North Adams comes to life.

Quotes From Reviews

*"**Disappearing Into North Adams** is a wonderful, personality-filled account of a period of change in a small New England mill town. Joe Manning has a poet's eyes and ears for the small things that matter: the inflections of speech, the loss of architectural artifacts, the threatening power of fresh ideas. The book is full of personal recollections that Manning wins through careful, caring interviews. Interwoven with the interviews, placed like fossils, are poems, photographs and short essays, most by Manning, who is a fine writer. The book has a gritty feel of the reality it absorbs. It is both a richly layered historical record and a piercing look forward."*
-Joseph Thompson, Director of the Massachusetts Museum of Contemporary Art

*"**Disappearing Into North Adams** is an impressive case study of what happened to a small American community in the name of urban development. A highly recommended example of specialized regional American history, Manning's engaging and informative text is enhanced throughout with period photography."*
-Midwest Book Review

*"**Disappearing Into North Adams** is a brilliantly executed and engaging account of a scrappy Massachusetts mill town attempting to remake itself. (It is) replete with real expressions and reflections from residents, an indication of how hard Manning listened to understand life's rhythms in North Adams. Manning's description of the coming to town of the Massachusetts Museum of Contemporary Art is an important account of the ways that life-long community residents, developers, and newcomers can work productively for the re-use of abandoned industrial space. (His) deft touches as an interviewer capture the personal hardships and life-altering confusions associated with job loss and economic dislocation. For anyone interested in learning more about the daily lives and thoughts of the people who built the country and then saw their handiwork threatened with extinction, **Disappearing Into North Adams** with Manning is a meaningful trip to take."*
-Robert Forrant, Associate Professor, Department of Regional Economic and Social Development, University of Massachusetts Lowell, as published in *The Public Historian*, Spring 2004.

"Joe Manning is a generous writer and listener. He invites us to walk the streets of one small city in America with him and compels us to listen to the stories this town has to tell. In the end, we learn as much about the author and about ourselves as we do about life in a specific time and place."
-Elizabeth Winthrop, author of over fifty works of fiction for adults and children, including *Dog Show*, *Island Justice*, *The Castle in the Attic* and *Dumpy La Rue*

How To Order *Disappearing Into North Adams*

Cost: $38.95 (price includes shipping).
Make check payable to Joe Manning.
Send to:
Joe Manning, Flatiron Press
575 Bridge Rd, Unit 9-1
Florence, MA 01062

All orders shipped Media Mail via US Postal Service.
For other shipping options, call or email the author.

Phone: 413-584-0679
Email: joe@sevensteeples.com
Website: www.sevensteeples.com

*Two dollars of each sale is donated to the North Adams Public Library.

ALSO FROM THE AUTHOR

I Love Baseball, by Steve Vozzolo and the Rookies, is a collection of fifteen original songs written by Joe Manning and Steve Vozzolo, plus an exciting new arrangement of "Take Me Out To The Ball Game," with the original verses that were written in 1908. All of the original songs have been accepted as part of the permanent collection of baseball music at the National Baseball Hall of Fame in Cooperstown, New York; and the album has been featured on ESPN.

Quotes From Reviews

*"I have collected quite a few CDs and cassettes with songs about the national pastime. While there are some wonderful compilations (with songs from a variety of artists) out there, without a doubt the best collection of baseball songs from a single artist is **I Love Baseball**, by Steve Vozzolo and the Rookies. The topics of the compositions (e.g., peanuts, the Hall of Fame, baseball cards) are wonderful, and Steve's vocals are perfectly matched to the material penned by Steve and Joe Manning."*
-Joe Mock, webmaster of BASEBALLPARKS.COM and author of *Joe Mock's Ballpark Guide*

*"**I Love Baseball** pleases on the first visit and delights on repeated visits. If you yearn for baseball's past and lament what we have lost, the album does not disappoint. Vozzolo and Manning know how to get to the heart of baseball's nostalgia and dreams. And to yours."*
-*NINE*: A Journal of Baseball History and Social Policy Perspectives

*"**I Love Baseball** is a wonderful, original album of baseball songs. The album really does go around the horn: from scouting ("They Say There's a Kid in Texas"), to nostalgia ("When Baseball Was Just a Game"), to the heartbreak of discovering missing parts of our childhood ("My Mother Threw Mine Away"). And it roams the entire country of baseball, from Little League and high school games ("Big Game Tonight"), to the minors ("Triple-A Blues"). I especially liked "Sometimes It Rains." I also enjoyed the sultry tribute to "The Peanut"('it's time the peanut took its rightful place in baseball history'). Some songs rock, like the lead-off "I Love Baseball"; others are soft and thoughtful like "Cooperstown" ('a place in our dreams where the stars look down.') "Black Diamond Days," which is about the Negro Leagues, is as cool as Papa Bell and jazzy as Satchel. Finally, there is "Take Me Out to the Ballgame." You hear the whole song, not just the refrain that everybody knows. This is a fine rendition, and might someday make Katy Casey as famous as the Casey who robbed Mudville of its joy. Highly recommended."*
-Gene Carney at Baseball1.com

<u>How To Order *I Love Baseball*</u>

Cost: $18.00 (CD) and $12.00 (tape). Price includes shipping.
Make check payable to Joe Manning.
Send to:
Joe Manning, Flatiron Press
575 Bridge Rd, Unit 9-1
Florence, MA 01062

All orders shipped First Class via US Postal Service.
For other shipping options, call or email Joe Manning.

Phone: 413-584-0679
Email: joe@sevensteeples.com
Website: www.sevensteeples.com

Gig At The Amtrak makes a great gift!

Order directly from the author.

<u>How To Order *Gig At The Amtrak*</u>

Cost: $22.95 (price includes shipping).
Make check payable to Joe Manning.
Send to:
Joe Manning, Flatiron Press
575 Bridge Rd, Unit 9-1
Florence, MA 01062.

All orders shipped Media Mail via US Postal Service.
For other shipping options, call or email the author.

Phone: 413-584-0679
Email: joe@sevensteeples.com
Website: www.sevensteeples.com